SQUARE PEGS CAN'T FIT INTO ROUND HOLES (OR CAN THEY?)

Fulton Books
Meadville, PA

Published by Fulton Books 2022

ISBN 979-8-88731-019-0 (paperback)
ISBN 979-8-88731-020-6 (digital)

Printed in the United States of America

SQUARE PEGS CAN'T FIT INTO ROUND HOLES (OR CAN THEY?)

Janet Reckard, LCSW

Toot was a square peg. He liked being square. It suited him just fine. Well, most of the time, anyway. But his parents and teachers constantly worried about him. They said things like "You're a duck out of water" or "You stick out like a sore thumb." You see, the world is made up of round holes. Being square, he didn't fit on the bus or in the classroom or in the gymnasium. He was out of place at family gatherings or at the mall. Other kids teased him and called him names like *weirdo* and *freak,* or they just ignored him.

Toot didn't understand that. He had two eyes, two ears, and two arms like everyone else. And all the other pegs looked different from one another too, like with their hair color and height, so why was he the only one who didn't fit in?

His grandfather used to tease him. He'd say, "Hey, Toot, that's spelled the same backwards and forwards, and if you turn it inside out, it spells Otto." And then he'd laugh like it was the funniest joke ever. Toot didn't really care because he liked being by himself. Well, most of the time, anyway.

One day, he read a book about snowflakes. It showed that no two snowflakes were ever alike. Even if there were a billion gazillion snowflakes, each one was different. Toot thought he would not be a freak or a weirdo if he were a snowflake. So he started reading everything he could about snowflakes. He Googled them on his laptop, checked out books at the library, and asked everyone if they knew anything about snowflakes. In fact, he could make any conversation about snowflakes. It usually went something like this:

KID: I love the color red.

TOOT: I love the color white. Snowflakes are white. Do you like snowflakes?

KID: Well, I...

TOOT: I love snowflakes. Did you know that no two snowflakes are ever alike?

KID: Cool, I...

TOOT: That's right. Each one is unique. That means they are all different.

KID: I like to play in the snow.

TOOT: If you play in the snow, you will ruin the snowflakes. There are a billion snowflakes in your front yard after only one inch of snow.

KID: Okay, well, see you later.

Toot tried to explain to everyone that pegs were like snowflakes because no two were alike. At first, pegs were interested, but soon, they started rolling their eyes or changing the subject or calling him Mr. Snowflake. His parents and teachers pleaded with him to stop talking about snowflakes. But he couldn't. Why, he wondered, didn't everyone see how magnificent snowflakes were?

Then in fifth grade he had a teacher named Mrs. Schney. She always smiled at him and noticed how good he was with some stuff like organizing things and doing diagrams, and she appreciated how much he knew about snow.

He started staying after school to talk to her. At first, they talked mostly about snow, but then he discovered that he liked talking to her about other stuff too. One day, as they were chatting, he noticed that she looked different.

He said, "Mrs. Schney, you look kind of oval."

She looked kind of surprised, but then she smiled and said, "Toot, you're right. I'll tell you a secret: I used to be oval. I didn't fit into any round holes. I felt sad and lonely. But I learned to put just enough pressure on myself to round out a little. I learned how to be more round when I needed to be, like at school, but when I'm at home or around pegs that I'm really comfortable with, I let my oval out."

Toot's eyes got wider. "Do you think you could teach me how to do that?" he asked.

"Well," she said, "for some reason, being round really seems important to pegs, so the world is made of round holes. But let's talk about snowflakes. It's true that each one is marvelous and unique by itself, but have you noticed that snowflakes can turn into wonderful creations when they blend together? They can turn into snow castles or snow forts or snow children."

She told him she would share the secrets she had learned about blending with others but still staying unique. Together they observed how pegs communicated in a group. They would do things like look at each other in the eyeballs, ask questions, listen to the answer, and make a comment about someone else's topic. Then they practiced doing that in their own conversations.

As he was practicing, Toot noticed something very interesting: his sides began to round out ever so slightly. His mom noticed it too and told him that his rough edges were beginning to smooth out. But not so much that he was round. Just enough to fit into some of the round holes when he wanted to.

Like when he wanted to get a job to earn some money. During the interview with the boss, he remembered to look at his eyeballs and answer his questions and not talk about snow. It must have worked because he got the job, and they actually *paid* him to play on computers in his own cubicle. He had finally found a square hole that he could fit into perfectly. Of course, he still had to round out sometimes, like when he ordered pizza for somebody's birthday. He rounded out his rough edges by eating a piece of pizza, looking at eyeballs when someone spoke to him, and asking a question or making a comment about what they were talking about.

Pegs seemed to like that. They started to call him Otto because he was rounded off on the outside but he still had his edges on the inside. Then he could go back to his cubicle and let his square out. At home, he could be totally his square self, like eating mac and cheese for dinner every night and making sure his books were organized alphabetically and continuing his research on polar explorers and avalanches. But when he was around other people, like at his job, he rounded out just a little bit. For example, he made sure he changed his shirt every day and took a shower (yuck!) because that was what the round pegs expected. It was a small price to pay to get paid for playing on the computer in his own cubicle.

He still liked being squarish, but he could decide how and when to round out a few rough edges when he needed to fit into a roundish hole. He even met a few other pegs who weren't really

round. Not exactly like him but kinda squarish or ovalish or starish. His friend the star peg had also learned to round off some of his rough points when he needed to. In fact, he noticed that none of the other pegs were exactly perfectly round. Just roundish.

Toot would always be a square peg, but that was okay. There was room in the world for all shapes, and shapes can round off a few edges when they want to fit into the roundish world without losing their uniqueness.

About the Author

Janet Reckard, LCSW, was a school social worker for many years and was part of a multidisciplinary team that diagnosed and worked with children on the spectrum.

She is currently retired from school practice but continues her private clinical practice. She raised three children and currently lives in Bloomington, Illinois, with her husband and menagerie.

Jim Reckard is a high school art teacher and photographer. He lives in Bloomington, Illinois, with his wife, Janet, and they enjoy traveling around the world.